WRITE FOR SUCCESS

Jim Mack

Heinemann

www.heinemannlibrary.co.uk
Visit our website to find out more information about Heinemann Library books.

To order:
☎ Phone +44 (0) 1865 888066
🖷 Fax +44 (0) 1865 314091
🖳 Visit www.heinemannlibrary.co.uk

Heinemann Library is an imprint of Capstone Global Library Limited, a company incorporated in England and Wales having its registered office at 7 Pilgrim Street, London, EC4V 6LB – Registered company number: 6695582

Heinemann is a registered trademark of Pearson Education Limited, under licence to Capstone Global Library Limited

Text © Capstone Global Library Limited 2009
First published in hardback in 2009
Paperback edition first published in 2011

Edited by Harriet Milles, Megan Cotugno, and Rachel Howells
Designed by Philippa Jenkins and Hart MacLeod
Original illustrations © Pearson Education Limited by Clare Elsom
Picture research by Elizabeth Alexander and Maria Joannou
Production by Alison Parsons
Originated by Modern Age Repro House Ltd
Printed and bound in China by South China Printing Company Ltd.

ISBN 978 0 431 11242 8 (hardback)
13 12 11 10 09
10 9 8 7 6 5 4 3 2 1

ISBN 978 0 431 11258 9 (paperback)
15 14 13 12 11
10 9 8 7 6 5 4 3 2 1

British Library Cataloguing-in-Publication Data
Mack, Jim
Write for success. - (Life skills)
808'.02
A full catalogue record for this title is available from the British Library.

Acknowledgements
We would like to thank the following for permission to reproduce photographs: © Alamy pp. **9** (John Rensten), **47** (Tetra Images); © Corbis pp. **5** (Ladislav Janicek/ Zefa), **7** (Charles Gupton), **12** (Sherri Barber/ NewSport), **37** (Ajax/ Zefa), **38** (Bettmann); © Getty Images pp. **23** (Blend Images/ Shalom Ormsby), **41** (Yellow Dog Productions/ Riser); ©Photolibrary pp. **19** (Foodpix), **45** (Bob Winsett); © Rex Features pp. **11** (David Lapper), **20** (Everett Collection), **49** (Peter Brooker); © TopFoto pp. **16** (Richard Lord/ The Image Works), **33** (Bob Daemmrich / The Image Works).

Cover photograph of man with Post-It notes™ reproduced with permission of ©2008 Masterfile Corporation (Edward Pond).

We would like to thank Tristan Boyer Binns for her invaluable help in the preparation of this book.

Every effort has been made to contact copyright holders of material reproduced in this book. Any omissions will be rectified in subsequent printings if notice is given to the Publishers.

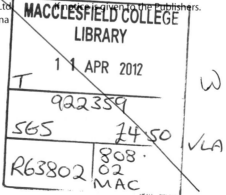

Contents

SKILLS TO LAST A LIFETIME 4

A QUICK LOOK AT GRAMMAR 6

GETTING STARTED................. 14

WRITING A RESEARCH REPORT..... 21

WRITING AT SCHOOL 27

WRITING ESSAY-STYLE ANSWERS .. 32

WRITING ABOUT LITERATURE...... 36

CREATIVE WRITING 40

WRITING FORMAL LETTERS 42

SPEECH WRITING 46

QUIZ RESULTS.....................50

20 THINGS TO REMEMBER 51

FURTHER INFORMATION.......... 52

GLOSSARY 54

INDEX............................ 56

Some words are printed in bold, **like this**. You can find out
what they mean by looking in the glossary.

Skills To Last A Lifetime

Good writing skills are essential in day-to-day **communication**. Our world thrives on people being able to communicate. Sometimes the written word can work better than the spoken word to get a point across. Most people write every day – using email, text messages, instant messages, and even little notes. The goal of written communication is to be sure that what you write is understood. To do this, your message must be clear, and have a purpose. A good writer will be able to pass on an idea or thought without confusion. However, most people are not born good writers. Just like anything else, it takes skills and practise.

Getting The Habit

Good writing is an acquired habit, like brushing your teeth. It's good for you, and in time it will become second nature. By mastering writing skills, you will be able to do well in school and later in the workplace. Every day you prepare for your future, so by picking up some writing skills now, you'll already have a head start for what lies ahead.

Schoolwork now focuses a lot on writing, and will continue to do so. It's important to learn good writing skills to do well on your assignments, succeed at school, and eventually land your dream job.

Many employers view writing skills as very valuable. Someone skilled in writing can do research and communicate his or her findings in a clear, understandable way. Good writers can organize their information in order to communicate and get their messages across. A competent writer shows that they are an organized person who can do the work it takes to succeed .

TIP

A big part of good writing is drafting, editing, and rewriting your message. Not everything comes out perfect the first time, so you have to rework it until it looks and sounds informative and clear.

From prehistory to history

The time before written language is now known as "prehistory." This term means the time before history, before the written records that humankind now uses to tell its story.

The first attempts to communicate using images can be traced back to prehistory when cave men would use sharpened stones and paints to carve and draw various pictures of their daily life onto the walls of the caves they inhabited. Later, more complex forms of pictorial writing, like the hieroglyphics of ancient Egypt, came into use. Eventually most cultures developed written languages using words and sentences.

For many years, communication over great distances relied on writing. It was first sent by messengers, on foot, horseback, or boat, later by train, and then by automobiles and planes. The telegraph system, using coded pulses called "Morse Code" to spell out messages and send them along a wire over great distances, came into use in the 1840s. The telephone wasn't invented until 1876. So, for most of recorded history, writing was the most common form of long-distance communication.

Modern technological advances have given us Internet-based ways to communicate, but most of this is still done through the written word. Communication through the spoken word is usually around only long enough for one person to hear it. The writing you do today has the potential to outlive you and still exist thousands of years in the future.

Egyptian hieroglyphics are one of the most ancient forms of writing. Pictorial symbols were used to describe objects, concepts, or sounds.

A Quick Look At Grammar

Understanding **grammar** is the foundation of all success in writing. So, let's have a quick grammar refresher to get warmed up.

WHAT IS GRAMMAR?

There are three styles of grammar: casual, conversational, and formal. Know your situation. Think about how you talk casually with friends, or how you speak when you first meet someone new and you're trying to get to know them. Then think about how you communicate with a teacher or other person of authority. You speak differently in each situation.

The same goes with writing. In most cases, you need to avoid the casual grammar style in your writing. You will be blending the conversational and formal styles to sound intelligent and for the text to read smoothly.

Now that you know the styles of grammar, let's talk about some of the basics of grammar. Here are some definitions for you to refer to when you are writing.

SOME PARTS OF SPEECH

Subject—the subject of any sentence you write is who or what you're talking about. It is usually a noun, which is a person, place, or thing. The subject can also be a pronoun (he,

she, him, her, it, etc.). *"Emily enjoys watching football. Her favorite team is in first place."* The subject of the first sentence is "Emily"(noun). In the second sentence, "Her" (pronoun) is the subject.

Verbs are the core of a sentence, the "doing" word. They are the engine that makes a sentence go. *"Dan hit several long drives at the golf course."* "Hit" is the verb.

Linking verbs are often called "being verbs" as they generally describe the state of the noun. These verbs form a "link" between two connected ideas in the same sentence. In the sentence *"Karen seemed upset.",* the linking verb is "seemed." The linking verb can link the object to an adjective, noun, or pronoun. "Upset" is an adjective describing Karen in the sentence *"Karen seemed upset."*

It is fine to use informal language when talking with friends, but think carefully before using it in your writing.

DID YOU KNOW?

Grammar is the word in Latin for "learning." Primarily, this refers to learning to read and write. The term "Grammar School" comes from the early era when schools mainly taught reading and writing. Although there are still schools called grammar schools, the word "grammar" now refers to the proper way to construct and use language.

Getting it Wrong

Slang is informal or playful use of language. It is looked down upon in written work as it can often come across as vague, abusive, or vulgar. Avoid slang in your writing if you want it to be understood properly and sound educated.

Linking verbs and pronouns—using a pronoun to complete the link is a little more difficult. Here's an example using a pronoun: *"The weakest link is she."* Sounds a little odd, doesn't it? That's because it is a very formal style. You may be used to using sentences like that casually. The incorrect way to say the same sentence is, *"The weakest link is her."*

A good way to check your sentence when linking to a pronoun is to reverse it. *"She is the weakest link."* Now try, *"Her is the weakest link."* "Her" and "him" are possessive pronouns that cannot be used without a noun (for example, "her idea" or "his answer"). So, using "she" is the correct choice!

Action verbs—these are the exciting verbs. Any verb that is not "being" is an action verb. They're labelled "action" because something happens. Make your writing worth reading and try to use as many different kinds of these powerful verbs as you can. *"My friend danced until her shoes broke."* "Danced" is the action verb. Action verbs even occur when not a lot of action is happening. *"I sleep eight hours every night."* Believe it or not, "sleep" is an action verb!

Object—even though action verbs can be exciting, if you're only combining them with a subject that can be pretty boring, such as *"Stacey waved"* or *"John shouted"*, an object is needed to better explain what is happening to the action. The action is then directed at the object. There are two main kinds of objects, direct objects and indirect objects. In the sentence *"Stacey wildly waved at Jared from across the street."* "Stacey" is the subject. The action verb is "waved." "Jared" is the direct object in the sentence because he is receiving the action of waving. Indirect objects are a little different. An indirect object will come before a direct object in a sentence. *"Since he was confused,*

• CHECKLIST •

Common linking verbs
Some commonly used linking verbs are:

am	are	is	was
were	will	be	shall
has	been	have	should
must			

(all parts of the verb to *be*)

look	sound	taste	smell
feel	appear	seem	grow
remain	stay.		

Jared shouted Stacey a question to ask what was wrong." "Jared" is the subject. "Shouted" is the action verb. "Stacey" is the indirect object. "Question" is the direct object.

Spice it up

Adjectives are words that describe a noun or pronoun. For example, in the phrase *"hot peppers,"* "hot" is the adjective and "peppers" is the noun. Adjectives add flavour to nouns and pronouns. Find the noun or pronoun and simply use a descriptive word to better explain it. Usually you can just ask a "What?" question to identify the adjective, like, *"What kind of pepper is it?"* The adjective "Hot" is the answer.

Adverbs are words that describe a verb. In the phrase *"perfectly cooked"*, "perfectly" is the adverb and "cooked" is the verb. Adverbs answer the questions: How? When? Where? Why? How was it done? Most adverbs end in "ly."

Adjectives are descriptive words that will make your writing more interesting. You don't have to directly experience the thing you are writing about!

9

STRUCTURE OF WRITING

Use complete sentences

All your sentences should be complete. A complete sentence has a subject and verb pair that work together. It should also express a complete, clear thought or piece of information. Incomplete sentences are known as fragments, phrases, or **dependent clauses**.

Paragraphs

Each paragraph in a piece of written work is almost like a mini paper or essay. Usually a paragraph will deal with one distinct idea or topic. It can be as short as a few sentences. A good paragraph will always have a topic sentence, followed by other supporting sentences. In a paper or essay, each paragraph will address its own main point. All the paragraphs will then relate back to the central theme or **thesis** of the paper.

SOME PUNCTUATION ADVICE

Using apostrophes

Who does it belong to? Apostrophes can be used to show **possession**. If a boy has a red ball, you would say, *"That boy's ball is red."* That would be an example of **singular** possession because there is only one boy. If there is more than one person in possession of something, you would put the apostrophe after the "s" to show **plural** possession, for example, *"The boys' ball is red."* or *"The girls' bathroom is closed for repairs."*

Apostrophes get a little tricky with the word "its." When "its" is used as a **contraction** of the words "it" and "is," the apostrophe is used to show this and represent the letters that have been left out. This means that when "its" is used to show possession, no apostrophe is added.

Getting it Right

Here is an example of a paragraph with a good introductory topic sentence, followed by three supporting sentences:

Bicycles are a great form of transportation. People of all ages can ride bicycles for both short and long distances. Bicycles are friendly to the environment because the only fuel they need is the strength in your legs. Everyone should own a bicycle.

Getting it **Wrong**

Here is an example of a paragraph with incomplete sentences and bad punctuation. It also deals with too many ideas, without fully developing any:

Bikes are bad. They may be friendly to the environment. But they are dangerous. Cyclist's never obey the rules of the road. Cars powered by electricity are the future.

Don't get stressed about your writing! Breaking essays down into manageable paragraphs is a good way to get started.

11

Commas and meaning

Commas can change the meaning of what is trying to be said. This is why it is so important to think carefully about how they are used.

Two commas can be used to separate off information that is not **essential** to the rest of the sentence. This means that when the text between two commas is removed, the sentence can still be understood as it was intended. *"All the players, who have been practising hard all season, want to get more playing time."* The information the sentence tells us is that all the players want to get more playing time. The commas separate off the extra information that they have all been practising hard as well.

If the text between the commas is removed, it still means "All the players want to get more playing time." However, if we remove the commas entirely, we have this: *"All the players who have been practising hard all season want to get more playing time."*

Without the commas, all the information becomes essential in creating the meaning of the sentence. The meaning now seems to be that only the few players who have been working hard want more playing time, while the original sentence with commas said that ALL the players want more playing time. The commas changed the sentence from referring to the entire team, to just talking about a few members of the team.

Grammar can change the meaning of a sentence. Removing commas may result in talking about just one or a few players, when you want to discuss all of them.

• CHECKLIST •

Here are some comma basics:

- Commas symbolize a pause, so a reader knows to separate information. Imagine taking a breath every time you see a comma.

- Always use commas if you are writing a sentence that contains a list of three or more items, for example, *"The ingredients are milk, honey, sugar, flour, and eggs."*

- Unless you are listing things, don't use a comma to separate complete thoughts (sentences). Complete thoughts can be grouped together into one sentence using conjunctions, such as "and", "or", and "but." *"Read this book, and you'll see how important writing is to your future success."* In this example a comma was used with the conjunction "and" to combine two complete thoughts.

- When two complete thoughts are grouped together as one sentence without a conjunction, only a semi-colon, not a comma, should be used to separate them: *"Read this book; you'll see how important writing is to your future success."*

PRACTISING GOOD GRAMMAR

1. What are the three styles of grammar?
a) correct, incorrect, and slang
b) conventional, formal, and informal
c) casual, conversational, and formal

2. What is the core of a sentence?
a) the verb
b) the object
c) the punctuation

3. What is another name for linking verbs?
a) action verbs
b) being verbs
c) doing verbs

4. A conjunction should be found at the beginning of a sentence.
a) true
b) false

Check page 50 to check your answers.

GETTING STARTED

Once you have refamiliarized yourself with some of the basics of grammar and punctuation, you can think about how to get started.

PREPARATION

It is very difficult to just sit down and start writing. It's similar to trying to drive a car with no petrol. Without fuel you are not going to get very far. With writing, your fuel is preparation. Before you start preparing, you are going to need an idea.

Do you have any ideas?

First, identify what kind of writing you are attempting. Is it a paper in essay style, a report, a letter, or a speech? Do you want to inform, persuade, or just entertain your readers? Once the type of writing you are doing and its purpose is established, choose your topic. This will be the focus that will drive the content of your writing.

Free writing

Free writing is an easy way to let your ideas flow; just start writing anything that comes to your mind. It doesn't have to relate to or mean anything. Here's an example of how a piece of free writing can lead to a good idea:

"I'm sitting at a desk. I'm writing words just to write them. I hope I have an idea somewhere in my brain. Let's see. What am I going to do today? Maybe I'll go for a bike ride in the park. Animals are in the park. I like animals. I wonder if there are any endangered animals in the park. Endangered animals!"

Getting it Right

Sometimes the topic you need to write about will be given to you. However, sometimes you will need to come up with a good idea yourself. Finding a suitable topic is often harder than it sounds. Focus on particular areas you are interested in or would like to learn more about. Once you have several ideas, examine each one separately and write down anything you can think of that is related to them. Two of the best ways to come up with ideas are free writing and brainstorming.

Brainstorming

Pick any of the ideas that came out in your free writing that might be a topic you can write about. Write that idea in the middle of the page, and draw a circle around it. Think of that as your main cloud or eye of the storm. Now draw lines from your main idea to branch off into other clouds. These new ideas or words will relate to the main cloud. Don't stop until you have a paper filled with storm clouds of mini ideas to support your main idea.

Take a look at your brainstorm. On a separate piece of paper start writing down a list of all the solid points that came out of your brainstorm. If you have a lot of ideas, focus on those most related to your main topic. This separate piece of paper will be the beginning of your research **notes**. You can now expand these notes even further by researching your ideas in a library, or just asking friends and family for more information.

Once you start brainstorming, you may be surprised at how many ideas you come up with!

RESEARCH

Research is a major part of most types of writing. You can use many sources to find information related to your topic. Remember: Don't depend on your memory. Take notes and write down the source. Don't be stingy with your source information. If it is a book, write down all the publishing information (title, author, publisher, place, and year of publication), as well as the number of the page where the information was found.

Getting it Right

If you don't write information down, you'll forget it or remember it inaccurately. So, write down everything you research, and pay particular attention to key points and facts. At the same time make sure you make a record of the sources where you found the information. This will save you a lot of time when you have to **cite** your sources or provide a **bibliography**.

Interviewing a professional person, such as a lecturer or doctor, is another good research method. Make the most of this experience by taking good notes.

TIP

Websites that end in *.edu*, *.gov*, and *.org* are usually reputable and reliable. Be careful with websites that end in .com. These web sites are **commercial**. Make sure they contain properly referenced information and are not just an excuse for product advertisements.

Information online

Start with the Internet. You can find lots of information online, including from almanacs and encyclopedias. However, you shouldn't do all your research online. It is good to use a variety of sources for most research reports, including books, newspapers, and magazines.

Library research

After you've made some progress online, it's time to head to the library. Sometimes you can save time if the catalogue for your school library or local public library is online and you can check in advance for books you might want to use. As well as books on the subject, other materials you might want to look for are almanacs, atlases, encyclopedias, government publications, magazines, and newspapers.

Don't be scared if you aren't used to library research. There's always someone to help if you ask, but don't expect the library staff to find everything for you.

In most libraries you can print out and photocopy materials as well as taking notes. Always record all the bibliographical information from the sources you use. If you are using a web page, record the URL as well as the creation or modification date.

Check with your teacher on how your references should be cited and how to structure your bibliography. You need complete bibliographical information in order to cite your sources or you won't be able to use them.

"You have to have a source, and if you don't have something you can cite from an original source, in the original language … you're not true."

William H. McNeill

CREATING AN OUTLINE

You have a big pile of notes, so what now? Well, it's time to put them all in order. The best way to do this is to make an **outline**.

Benefits of an outline

An outline helps you organize and order all your notes and research. It helps you find new connections between the information you may not have noticed before. It also helps you weed out all the material that doesn't really fit.

What to include

The outline will consist of your topic, all the subtopics related to it, and any backup information you find. Your outline is the skeleton or frame of your paper. You have to decide what information will go in the introduction of the paper, what will go in the body, and what will go in the conclusion. It's a bit like a puzzle. You have to put all the pieces together under general headings. Then you move them around until they fit together and make sense.

Reviewing

Don't try to write your whole paper on your outline; just include the main points to guide you as you write. Revise your outline several times. The more polished it is, the easier it will be

• CHECKLIST •

Different ways to organize an outline:

- By purpose/intent
- Chronologically: historical event order
- By cause-and-effect relationships
- In a step-by-step process
- By defining/analyzing
- By comparing/contrasting
- Presenting an argument
- By theme

to write your paper. Keep all your old outline versions in case you need to refer to them.

Practise making an outline. Pick a favourite food, and explain in outline form why it is your favourite. The example outline on the next page is for a ham and cheese sandwich.

1

Introduction
- Ham and cheese is the best sandwich
- Tastes great
- A cheap meal

2

Body
- Easy to make
- Bread
- Ham
- Cheese
- Healthy
- Protein
- Dairy
- Multi-grain bread

3

Conclusion
- Great snack or meal for people on the go
- Making a lunch was never this easy

YOUR THESIS

After you've completed your outline, it's time to come up with the thesis that will appear in your introduction. The thesis is the statement of what you are trying to say in your paper. It will consist of your main idea and where you plan to take it. The majority of the rest of your paper will be in support of your thesis statement. To start with, try to write it in one sentence. Make it short, compact, and strong.

TIP

A strong way to declare your thesis is through a definite statement of opinion or belief: *"I believe the Lost City of Atlantis existed."* Another way is to ask a question: *"Are UFO sightings real?"* You can also express or support a theory: *"I support the theory that the Loch Ness Monster is a hoax."*

The view you take in your thesis is up to you, as long as you support it with strong evidence. Robert K. Wilson took this photograph of the "Loch Ness Monster" in 1934 - only he knows whether or not it is a hoax!

WRITING A RESEARCH REPORT

The idea has been found and the topic decided on. The research has been done and the notes taken and referenced. The outline has pulled all the ideas into a plan and the thesis statement has been written. All this preparation has made you ready to write.

THINGS TO THINK ABOUT

Be logical and organized

When you start writing, make sure your report flows in a **logical** order so that it makes sense to whoever is reading. Each paragraph should begin with a topic or subtopic that is supported by the following sentences. If there are several areas of support, explain how they relate to each other as well as to the topic. Finally, finish your essay with a strong conclusion.

Choose your words carefully

Dress your words to impress. Your writing piece can have some flavour, so try to enhance it with sprinkles of strong, colourful words, but make sure you know exactly what they mean so they're used correctly. The words you use don't have to be difficult, but they have to be appropriate for the subject you are writing about. Remember that some topics may have their own unique words or technical language that you need to show familiarity with. Good word choices reflect the effort put into the research and writing by proving there is something intelligent to be said. A good **thesaurus** and dictionary are useful tools to help you make better word choices.

Using a thesaurus

Using a thesaurus can be very useful when choosing vocabulary. There are several reasons why. First, it can be difficult to avoid using the same word in a sentence or paragraph. Repeating a word makes it seem like you don't have a good vocabulary or understanding of your topic. Second, a thesaurus can help you find a more specific word. You could be writing about the scientist and inventor Thomas Edison, saying "The light bulb was a *good* idea." In this context, the word *good* is weak and unspecific. What about *brilliant*, *remarkable*, or *ingenious*? Third, a thesaurus can also give the opposite meaning of a word, which is more specific than just adding *not* or *un* to a word. Rather than say "He was *not proud* of what he had done", *ashamed* may have a meaning closer to what you are trying to say.

Sentence structure is important

Sentences should be written to blend **informative** speech and normal conversation. Short, **bland** sentences will make the text seem like it was written by a robot. On the other hand, long, rambling sentences are difficult to understand even when they are grammatically correct. A happy medium needs to be found.

Your words should be read almost as if the person can hear you speaking them. Here's a robotic example: *"I went to the shop. They didn't have milk. I left."* It can be expressed much better than that. How about: *"I ran over to the supermarket on West Road. After frantically looking for milk, I gave up and left empty handed."*

Organize those notes

Your research notes form the **foundation** of your attempt to communicate your findings and thoughts. Using your notes you can come up with **insights** into the topic.

Take a look at your outline, and then analyze all your research. Everything relevant should fit somewhere in your outline. If you find something that doesn't seem to fit in, get rid of it.

This is a good time to check that all the information you are going to use from your notes is fully referenced. You will need to cite all sources and research material.

You don't want to **plagiarize** anything you write, not even by mistake. If the ideas aren't yours, then you must give the original author credit. Even though the ideas are not all yours, having done thorough research with well cited sources will only make the report stronger.

TIP

Get a report or essay rolling by using one of these openings:

- Ask a thoughtful question.
- List the main points to introduce a topic.
- Start with a funny story.
- Begin with a dramatic statement.
- Use a quote from an expert related to your topic.
- Use a fresh point of view that you came up with yourself.

Getting it
Wrong

Plagiarism is stealing someone's words or ideas and claiming they are your own. It can be a serious offence resulting in a failing grade, getting expelled, or even getting arrested. If you are using another source you can never copy it word for word unless you acknowledge that it is someone else's work. Remember, changing a few words in someone else's sentence does not make it your words. If you need to use a source in your report, whether it's word for word or just a specific idea, always cite your source. Use quotation marks to alert the reader that what they are reading is someone else's words. Here is an example: Thomas Jefferson once said, "Honesty is the first chapter in the book of wisdom." Ask your teacher to provide information about what format your citations and bibliography should take.

Ask a teacher or librarian if you are unsure about how to cite your sources.

WRITING THE FIRST DRAFT

Before you start writing your first draft, make sure all your notes are organized in the order of your outline so you can get to all your research easily. Take a deep breath. Focus on your thesis, and then just start from the top of your outline and make your way down one section at a time. Go over all the relevant notes for each area of your outline as you go. **Summarize** or **paraphrase** from your notes and research materials. Make the writing sound like it's coming out in your voice, but do not make it too informal or too stilted. Feel free to quote directly from any resources; just make sure you cite them in the text and include them in your bibliography.

Revise your draft

Read through the first draft of your report for any obvious errors. Make sure all your content follows your outline. If it doesn't, now is the time to arrange it so it does.

"Writing the last page of the first draft is the most enjoyable moment in writing. It's one of the most enjoyable moments in life, period."

Nicholas Sparks

• CHECKLIST •

Check the report content:

- Do I have a clear and concise thesis statement?
- Does my report follow my outline?
- Does my supporting content have a logical order?
- Are all my sources cited properly?
- Have I proved my thesis with my supporting content?
- Are all my points clear?

Checking the writing:

- Do I have any spelling or grammatical errors?
- Do my paragraphs flow smoothly from one to the next?
- Are my paragraphs structured properly with topic sentences and support?
- Are my sentences complete?
- Are my quotations and citations accurate and formatted correctly?
- Is my conclusion clear and complete?
- Does the conclusion restate my thesis and provide a good closing explanation of the ideas I'm trying to get across?

THE FINAL DRAFT

All formal work like essays and research reports should be typed and printed on good paper. Reread your final draft carefully and proofread it for any errors. If possible, have a friend or relative look it over as well. The actual report should look good, too, so don't just shove it in your backpack. Turn in a clean report with no wrinkles, stains, or tears. Take pride in the presentation of the report. It represents your hard work.

Make sure you hand in a presentable final draft. All your hard work will be for nothing if the paper looks torn and messy.

• CHECKLIST •

Check your research report or essay obeys the following key points:

- Make sure it flows logically – you should have an introduction, main body, and conclusion.
- Keep organized research notes.
- Make sure all your research is relevant to your topic.
- Decide on a strong sentence structure.
- Use a thesaurus to liven up your text.
- Write a first draft before you attempt a final draft.
- Always cite your sources.
- Include a bibliography.

WRITING TECHNIQUE

1. Free writing means:
a) writing without looking down at the paper
b) letting your ideas flow and see what happens
c) getting a report written by someone else at no cost

2. If I take someone else's idea from a book and change a few words, I don't need to cite it.
a) true
b) false

3. A thesaurus can be useful if:
a) you don't know what a word means
b) you need to find another word with the same meaning
c) you want to sound more educated and intelligent

4. Using cited sources in your report will:
a) make it weaker
b) make it stronger
c) have no effect

Check page 50 to check your answers.

Writing At School

No matter where you go to school, there are two types of writing everyone will encounter. Research reports and essays are educational standards. The research report is designed with the goal of learning something new through in-depth research, while essays are more creative or are a demonstration of knowledge gained.

Research Reports

A research report is not as hard to write as you might think it is. Remember, you're researching material that already exists. A lot of the hard work has already been done for you. All you have to do is some detective work, examine all the evidence, and write up a report. Sound fun? It can be, particularly when you pick a topic that interests and challenges you.

TIP

If you have a choice about your topic, make sure you select something manageable. For example, if you choose the topic "The Solar System," you might find you cannot cover such an enormous subject within the length of your report. It could be better to choose one specific planet, like Venus or Saturn.

Layout of a research report outline

Your outline should consist of three main parts:

1

Introduction
Here you'll have your thesis and purpose. Ask yourself what you want to accomplish with this report. State your approach, and briefly explain how you plan to cover all the major points and areas of your report.

2

Body
Have at least three paragraphs that argue, support, or defend your topic position.

3

Conclusion
Refer back to your thesis. Summarize your arguments. Briefly explain how you came to your conclusion.

Persuasive essay

Have you ever had an idea you thought was better than someone else's idea? If you've had to **debate** with someone over whether or not you're right, then you know the person with the best supporting evidence usually wins out… unless you're debating with your mother over how late you can stay up on a school night! Usually whatever evidence or support you have in your favour will most likely never win that argument, but it doesn't hurt to try.

A persuasive essay can also be called an argument essay or an essay to convince. It uses logic and reason to show that one idea is better than the other. The goal of a persuasive essay is to get the reader to believe in what you have to say by accepting your point of view. You have to focus on selling your ideas, supported by good evidence.

When you have the option to choose your own topic, pick something you are either for or against. It's very important that the topic is debatable, meaning it can be argued from either side. It's easier to be convincing if the topic is something you are interested in and feel motivated to write about.

For or against?

Let's use the example of "Environmental Safety" as a good topic choice. Here are two points of view that could be used to write about this subject:

- Dumping waste in the ocean is good because it feeds fish and gives them new objects to swim around.
- Dumping waste in the ocean is bad because it kills fish and is very hazardous to underwater plant life.

An argument can be made about anything, but eventually it needs to be backed up with proof.

TIP

- To make an impact, you could start your essay with a quotation.
- Make a statement.
- Begin with a statistic or a fact.
- Ask a question.
- Be dramatic.
- Use a strange detail or weird fact to hook the reader.

Now brainstorm!

Once a topic is chosen, it's best to brainstorm it, research it, take notes, and make an outline. Brainstorm both sides of the argument. You'll only write about one side, but you still need to completely understand the other side to effectively argue against it.

Think of the other side of the argument as your opponent. It's important to know everything you can about your opponent. In your report you'll want to touch upon everything the opponent, the other side of the argument, can throw at you. For instance, if your topic relates to persuading people against smoking, the other side of the argument would claim that smoking causes no harm. You must be able to say exactly why that is not true.

Knowing your opponent's argument as well as your own will help you build an effective case.

CONS
- EXPLOITATION
- CONFINEMENT
- INADEQUATE FACILITIES
- UNNATURAL LIVES
- CRUELTY/ CAPTURE/ TRANSPORT

ZOOS

PROS
- CONSERVATION
- PUBLIC EDUCATION
- SCIENTIFIC RESEARCH
- NATURAL LIVES
- BREEDING PROGRAMMES

Evidence

Evidence is needed to **counter** the other side of the argument. Evidence can be found in facts and quotations. Obviously smoking is bad for you, but you'll need to do some research to prove it. Exact statistics on the problems caused by smoking can be very effective in proving your argument. Rely on hard facts, instead of truths. A truth is something that is believed by many, like the statement, *"Smoking is bad."* A fact is something more concrete, usually backed up by evidence. *"Eighty-seven percent of lung cancer cases are caused by smoking."* Statistics like this are useful evidence. They are even more impressive when they come from experts or well-respected sources. Make sure you cite the reference for such information. Relevant examples and **anecdotes** can also help your reader understand the points you are trying to get across.

- **Analyze:** Break down all opposing problems so the reader fully understands.

- Use **analogy:** Compare situations to something the reader understands and can identify with. For example, if you are trying to explain to teenage readers what having to pay higher taxes feels like to adults, you could say *"A tax increase is like getting less allowance for doing the same amount of chores."*

- **Compare/Contrast:** Briefly explain the similarities and differences in both sides of argument then attack from your point of view.

Layout of a persuasive essay outline

1 Introduction
- Present a firm opinion on a debatable topic.
- Provide background to establish a thesis.

2 Body
- Have at least three arguments in three separate paragraphs.
- Include supporting evidence in each paragraph.

3 Conclusion
- Summarize the main points of the argument.
- Restate the thesis and point of view.
- Close with a strong, convincing statement.

Getting it Wrong

Unsupported opinions will never win an argument. Do you like it when your parents or a teacher tells you to do something "because I say so"? No one does. However, that is what an unsupported opinion can seem to your readers. When you are writing to convince or persuade, the quality of your evidence, and how successfully you integrate it into your argument, is what your readers will have to weigh up in coming to their own decisions about the subject.

Make sure you have evidence to support your point of view. Getting angry or aggressive won't help!

Writing Essay-Style Answers

The entire point of essay-style tests and exams is just like it is for other tests: to demonstrate your understanding. In other words, your answers can show that you learned something. Remember, writing your answers for this kind of test is just like any other kind of writing, which means you have to prepare. It's also important to study for an essay exam the same way you would for any normal test. Go over the material you have learned, and ask yourself questions like, "What if I was asked about that? How would I answer? What information could I use to support my answer?"

Time is not on your side

Unless it's a take home test, you will only have a limited amount of time to finish the exam. However, writing under the pressure of time does not give you the excuse to write before you think. Some time for planning has probably been included in the time limit.

Some initial ideas

Scribbling down a few ideas or points before you start can be the difference between a good and a bad answer. Write quickly, but don't write so sloppily that your words are impossible to read. Being able to write quickly will give you more time to think about the questions.

Getting it Right

Writing less is often better than writing more in any situation, especially in an essay exam. Don't just ramble on, writing everything you can think of that relates to the question, hoping somehow you will stumble across the correct answer. Your teachers know the material so they will be looking for you to bring up key points to show what you've learned. A successful essay answer will contain specific information learned in class or examples gathered from assignments or other materials, such as required reading from textbooks.

• CHECKLIST •

- Study and Prepare: Exams usually are not a surprise, so you'll have ample time to get ready. Go over everything that you learned. An essay exam question will usually tie in main themes of the course. If there is more than one question, make sure you manage your time well in order to answer all the questions.

- Read and reread the essay question: Spend several minutes examining the question to make sure you understand it. Then start thinking critically about how it relates to what you've learned in class. Be sure to have an opinion and more importantly, be able to support that opinion.

- Make a quick outline: While you are thinking about the question, start writing down any points that come to mind that you want to make in your essay. Use a scrap piece of paper or just write in the margin. This will help you organize your ideas so when you start writing it flows in a logical order that makes sense to the reader. If an idea pops into your head, quickly write it down otherwise you could forget it.

Take a few minutes to think about the essay question before you start writing.

STRUCTURING AN ESSAY ANSWER

Introduction

Your introduction should use the information in the question along with your knowledge of the topic. Compose a brief thesis statement. Follow this with a brief description of the general points you want to make, and the importance of the opinion you will be supporting.

Support

Support is important. Your thesis needs to be backed up in the body of your paper with all the points that were laid out in your introduction. Use examples, facts, and other useful information that you learned in class to back up your points.

Conclusion

In your conclusion, summarize all the main points and explain how they tie into your thesis. A good conclusion will display you understood the question, answered it, and were able to relate it not only to the thesis but also to the main theme of what you had learned in class.

Proofread!

If you have time, always go back and check to make sure you covered everything. It is good to leave extra space between paragraphs in case you have to add anything at the last minute. Check spelling, grammar, and punctuation. Also make sure it makes sense. If there's any information that doesn't fit well into the thesis, it's okay to clearly cross it out (no need to scribble).

Is it right to keep endangered animals in zoos?

I believe that keeping endangered animals in zoos is necessary. Wild animals are at risk from poachers, and some animal species are dwindling so much that they may soon be extinct. Keeping animals like tigers, pandas, and gorillas in captivity is important because it is the only way we can preserve these unique species.

Let's take the case of the tiger. In the last 100 years tiger numbers have declined by 95 percent, which means there are currently less than 4,000 of these beautiful creatures still in the wild. They exist in isolated forest areas in parts of India, south-eastern China, the Russian Far East, and Indonesia. One of the reasons so few are left is because they are the victims of an illegal wildlife trade, which includes traditional Chinese medicine. Tiger bone has been used for hundreds of years as a treatment for arthritis. Traditional Chinese medicine now rejects the use of tiger bone as an ingredient in their remedies, but poaching still continues. Changing traditional attitudes towards these animals is difficult, so zoos need to exist to preserve important species like the tiger.

Zoos serve an important purpose in the modern world. We are becoming an increasingly urban society, but that does not mean we should not care about the world's endangered species. Although groups like the World Wildlife Federation are doing their best to put a stop to poaching, there is a limit to what they can do. History has shown how important animals species like the dodo have disappeared completely. At least we will have protected some of our animals in zoos.

[Information taken from the World Wildlife Federation website (www.worldwildlife.org)]

Getting it Right

One way to study for an essay test is to practise written arguments by brainstorming pairs of ideas, or likes and dislikes, against each other. Use a separate piece of paper for each side. For example, you could practise using the following pairs, or you could find ideas from the material you are going to be tested on and use this technique to study.

- Fruit vs. Vegetables

- Bikes vs. Skateboards

- Swimming vs. Running

"Say what you are going to say, say it, then say what you've said."

ESSAY EXPERT

1. **What are the three main parts of an outline?**
   a) the start, middle, and finish
   b) the introduction, body, and conclusion
   c) foundation, intermediate, and advanced

2. **What is the goal of a persuasive essay?**
   a) to convince the reader about something
   b) to confuse the reader
   c) to fool the reader into thinking you are right

3. **It is always best to choose a big topic for a research report because there will be lots of things to write about.**
   a) true
   b) false

Check page 50 to check your answers.

Writing About Literature

At school, one of the most common types of writing you will be asked to do is writing about **fiction** you have read, whether it be a **novel**, short story, or poem. This type of writing can take the form of an examination of the style and language of a poem, a book review, or even a research report on an author. Often, you are asked to be critical and give your opinion.

Writing Book Reviews

Most book reviews follow a similar pattern, but make sure you do it the way your teacher prefers. Once again, just like with research reports, preparation can be the key to writing a good book review.

Read through the instructions you have been given before you start reading so you know what to look for. Then, you can take notes as you read or, if you prefer, wait until you have finished the book and then make notes based on the requirements for the report. In most book reviews you first have to provide information about the book you read: its title, author, and publishing information. It's also a good idea to say how many pages long it is.

Plot and characters

Most book reviews need to have a brief summary of the plot and an explanation of who the main characters are. It is also useful to put the book in its **context**. Does the action take place in a foreign country or on another planet? Is it set at some other time in history, in the present, or in the future?

What do you think?

In a book review you have to say what you think about the book, praising the good parts and criticizing the things you think the author got wrong. The areas you like or dislike can relate to any aspect of the book, from its style of writing to the personalities of the characters.

While this will be based on your own opinions, it is always sensible to give reasons why you think what you do. For example, is it more interesting to your reader for you to say, *"I disliked the main character of the horse trader"*, or *"I disliked the main character of the horse trader, because he continually bullied the widow and her young son."*?

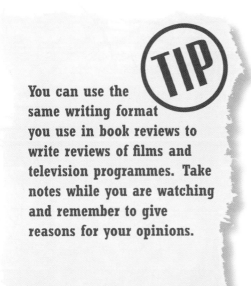

You can use the same writing format you use in book reviews to write reviews of films and television programmes. Take notes while you are watching and remember to give reasons for your opinions.

What is insight?

When you are writing about literature, one of the most important ways you can show you are familiar with and understand what you are writing is by demonstrating insight. Having insight means being able to see beyond the obvious ways of looking at something. It means that you have taken the trouble to really dig into it.

Researching for insight

Sometimes to get insight about something, you need to do research about the subject of a book, short story, or poem, or even about the life of the author. If a short story is about an orphan boy travelling across France during World War Two and you find out that the author himself had that experience, this information will give your writing insight.

As you read, try to think about the meaning of the words. This will help you analyze the text in your writing.

WRITING ABOUT POETRY

Poetry can often be very difficult to understand. The style, imagery, and forms of poems can make them very different from each other. Some writing about poetry is similar to book reviews in that you describe the poem and then say what you thought of it. Another kind of writing about poetry can focus on an examination of a group of poems by one poet. You can also compare and contrast two poems, either by the same poet or by two different authors. No matter which kind of writing about poetry you do, it is important to remember that you should show familiarity with the special language used to describe poetry.

REFERRING TO THE TEXT

Whatever kind of writing about literature you are doing, one of the most vital things is always to support your views by referring to the text. Giving examples to support what you say demonstrates that you really do understand the work and can back up your comments. See the "Getting it Right" box on the next page for an example of this.

This is an engraving of Robert Burns, created by William Harry Warren Bicknell.

Getting it Right

If you are writing about the poem " My Love is Like a Red, Red Rose" by the Scottish poet Robert Burns, you could say that Burns uses similes to develop the imagery of the poem. However, if you quote from those specific places where he uses similes (*"like a red, red rose"* and *"like the melodie/That's sweetly play'd in tune"*), you have provided evidence to back up your claim.

• CHECKLIST •

Poetry is described using many special terms. Here are some you can look up and then use when you next have to write about poetry.

- **Figures of speech:** alliteration, hyperbole, metaphor, simile, assonance, personification

- **Poetic forms:** sonnet, ballad, limerick, *haiku*, ode, epic

- **Structure:** verse, foot, meter, rhyme

A LOVE FOR LITERATURE?

1. **A book review should never give the opinions of the person who wrote it.**
   a) true
   b) false

2. **Which two of the following terms are figures of speech?**
   a) metaphor
   b) sonnet
   c) hyperbole
   d) free verse

3. **If you get insight about a piece of literature this means you:**
   a) have seen many different copies of it
   b) can use your knowledge to write with more understanding
   c) have permission to ask your friends what they think about it

CREATIVE WRITING

Some of the most rewarding writing you can do is the writing that comes from your own feelings and imagination. The term usually used for this is creative writing. This is because you have created it from your own original thoughts and ideas.

WRITING POETRY AND SHORT STORIES

At school, poetry and short stories are probably the most common types of creative writing you will be asked to do. However, it can be hard being creative at someone else's request. When you are trying to come up with ideas, remember that free writing and brainstorming can be useful here.

Sometimes with poetry, choosing a form, such as *haiku* or sonnet, can help you start writing. When you are studying a particular poet, your assignment might be to write a poem in the style of that poet. Ask yourself what form the poet uses and what figures of speech. Does he or she always write poems with a particular theme, such as nature?

With short stories, once you have come up with an idea, it is important to remember that any book or story is driven along by the strength of its plot and characters.

So, once again, the time spent thinking and preparing can be as important as the writing itself. What makes the characters and plots of the books or stories you really like outstanding? Can you use some of the same, or similar, ideas?

DIARIES, JOURNALS, AND PERSONAL BLOGS

Most of the writing that has been discussed so far puts you in the position of the researcher, the critic, or the imaginative author. With diaries, journals, and blogs, YOU are the subject.

Diaries are usually private and may contain very personal details of your feelings, hopes, and worries. A diary can be a way for you to make sense of events in your life by writing about them. Writing in a diary every day is also a good discipline and good writing practice. Journals are similar in that they are usually written regularly, like a diary, but they can relate to a specific subject or a special event, like a school trip.

Getting it Right

If the idea of writing for the stage or screen interests you, get out there and give it a go! Read as many famous plays as you can to find out how successful playwrights have structured their scenes and written effective dialogue (speech). If you are having trouble thinking up ideas for a play, a good start could be to adapt a children's fairytale for a school show. (Go to page 53 for more on playwriting.)

WRITING FORMAL LETTERS

Successful writing can have a considerable effect on your future. Writing to family and friends is not the only time you need to write letters. Sometimes finding a job requires writing a formal letter to an employer. Also, on various occasions during your life, you will almost certainly have to fill in job or college application forms, or prepare a CV.

FORMAL LETTERS

Inquiring about a job isn't the only reason to write a formal letter. A formal letter is used to request information as well as to give information. For example, a professional looking written complaint is more likely to be dealt with than a demanding verbal one.

There are several different ways to write a formal letter. The most common is called "block format." It's called block because the letter will contain blocks of text that are all aligned to the left of the page.

At the right-hand side of the letter will be the address of the sender. Below that on the left-hand side will be the block of the address of the person you are sending to, followed by the date. Then there will be a block of an opening salutation with an introduction. After that will be a block for the body, followed by a closing block. Finally there will be a block for the signature. Each block should be separated by a line of space.

For clarity, it's best to use a formal **font**, like Times New Roman or Palatino, with a font size of 12 points.

The greeting of a letter is called a salutation. It's always best to have a name to use in the salutation. So, if you know the name, use the appropriate title (Mr., Mrs., Miss, or Ms., Dr., etc.) followed by the last name only. For example, *"Dear Mr. Mack:"* If a name cannot be found use *"Dear Sir or Madam:"*

Miss or Ms.? TIP

Miss is used if you know for a fact the woman is single. Ms. is an acceptable way to refer to a single or married woman, or if you know it to be the woman's preference.

Finishing off

When ending a letter, it is customary to use *"Yours sincerely,"* followed by your signature. If you have put *"Sir or Madam"* in the salutation, use *"Yours faithfully,"* followed by your signature. Always sign the letter with a signature followed by your name either printed or typed out. Usually you only put a title for yourself if you think the reader will not be able to tell if you are male or female by your name.

How to lay out a block letter

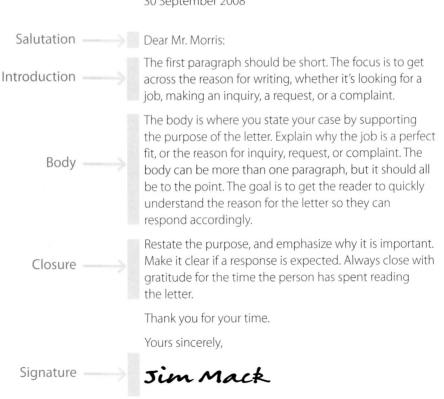

Jim Mack
172 Marlborough Road
Maidstone
Kent, ME14 1XQ

John Morris
86 Shout Street
Oxford, OX1 4LT
30 September 2008

Salutation ⟶ Dear Mr. Morris:

Introduction ⟶ The first paragraph should be short. The focus is to get across the reason for writing, whether it's looking for a job, making an inquiry, a request, or a complaint.

Body ⟶ The body is where you state your case by supporting the purpose of the letter. Explain why the job is a perfect fit, or the reason for inquiry, request, or complaint. The body can be more than one paragraph, but it should all be to the point. The goal is to get the reader to quickly understand the reason for the letter so they can respond accordingly.

Closure ⟶ Restate the purpose, and emphasize why it is important. Make it clear if a response is expected. Always close with gratitude for the time the person has spent reading the letter.

Thank you for your time.

Yours sincerely,

Signature ⟶ *Jim Mack*

James Mack

WRITING APPLICATIONS

Most applications for higher education and jobs require form filling. While many forms can now be completed online, you are still likely to have to do some in your own handwriting.

Again, preparation is the key to success. Whether a form is online or paper, read it carefully before you do anything. Check that you have all the information you need. Write out some of the longer answers on scrap paper and be sure you are happy with your spelling and grammar.

Look at the spaces available for the answers and consider if the replies you want to give will fit. If not, do the instructions say it is satisfactory to use extra paper? You will be judged not only on the quality of your answers, but also on your ability to follow the instructions and complete the form in a legible, grammatical, and accurate way.

A **cover letter** should go with most applications.

TIP

Never leave blank spaces when filling in a form. It is hard for the person reading it to know if you have forgotten something. It is always best to draw a line through a section you have no answer for, or write "Does not apply" in the space.

CVs

A CV **(Curriculum Vitae)** is a short personal data form including educational and job history. Some applications require that you provide a CV.

There are many useful Internet sites that contain advice on creating CVs and have samples for you to look at. School counsellors and career advisors can also help you come up with the perfect CV.

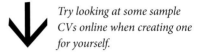

Try looking at some sample CVs online when creating one for yourself.

Speech Writing

So your words look good on paper, but how will what you write sound like coming out of your mouth? Speech writing presents a whole new set of challenges. A speech can be about anything from politics to a **toast** said at a wedding or birthday. It can be persuasive, informative, or both. Speech writing is a **culmination** of everything you've learned so far. It's also the most fun.

GET PREPARED

Giving a speech is like giving a performance. It's a blend of good writing and being able to speak in a natural way. There is no reason to be nervous. Anyone can write and then give a speech. All it takes is a little bit of preparation. There are three main things to think about before writing a speech: occasion, audience, and purpose.

DID YOU KNOW?

Jon Favreau is only 26 years old, yet his speech writing skills so impressed the US presidential candidate, Barack Obama that he hired Favreau to be his head speechwriter. While many people of his age are still trying to work out what they will do with their lives, Favreau is writing speeches that could make history!

• CHECKLIST •

- *Occasion*—first work out what kind of speech to give. Is it part of a persuasive speech for a school debate, or is it for a special occasion like a birthday or a wedding anniversary?
- *Audience*—think about the audience. For example, if it's for school, try to tackle an issue of interest to your classmates, like MP3 downloads. It is important to always keep the audience in mind.
- *Purpose*—set some goals for the speech. For example, for a speech on MP3 downloading, your goals could be write a speech that has humour, with a serious tone, backed by facts.

Writing your speech

Speech writing can be a little less formal than other types of writing. The key to writing a good speech is to write like you talk. To do this you will have to structure your sentences differently than if you were writing an essay. An easy way to accomplish this is to make a list of points you intend on making in your speech. Choose words you would normally use. The goal is to write as if you were talking so when you give the speech it will sound natural. Try talking about each point out loud. Once you have gone through your points several times, sit back down, and write out what you have been saying.

You don't need to memorize your speech completely, but reading it straight from your notes won't impress your audience.

Attention getter, body, and closing

Write your speech to grab the attention of the audience right from the start. Be loud, funny, or gravely serious. Ask a question or use a quotation. You want all eyes on you. Keep the audience's interest. The body of a speech should be written to contain a purpose and everything that the audience needs to know. Clearly build up from each point to the next. Remember that unless you become famous, your speech won't appear where it can be reread. It has to be understood first time through. Write the closing to be even stronger than the opening. Summarize all the main points, and leave the audience wanting more.

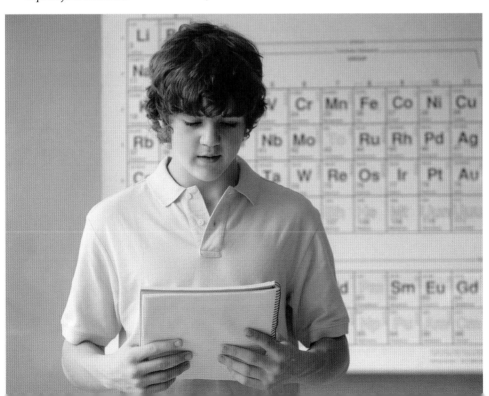

WRITING FOR SUCCESS

The fundamental purpose of writing is to communicate ideas that need to be understood or remembered. Without writing, it would be extremely difficult to remember anything from grocery lists to world history.

Writing is a great skill to master, and anyone can do it. To become a successful writer you must first understand some basic techniques and then practise them. There are many different forms of writing, but with the exception of some creative writing, they all have a basic structure with an introduction, body, and conclusion just like a story has a beginning, middle, and end.

PREPARATION, PREPARATION, PREPARATION

Good writing comes from research, critical thinking, and revision. Ideas may seem to come out of nowhere, but good writing does not. Preparation must be done before writing can even begin. It is the key element in the writing process. Following all these steps will ensure you are ready to create a great piece of writing.

Writing is one of the best ways to voice an opinion, but solid opinion can only be supported after thorough research. An opinion will only get stronger as you go through the process of taking notes all the way down to revising a final draft. The words of a good writer will be able to persuade his or her readers to understand clearly a specific point of view using facts, evidence, and a convincing conclusion.

WRITING FOR YOUR FUTURE

School is not the only situation that requires writing. As you grow older, your future may depend heavily on your ability to communicate easily and accurately through the written word. A formal letter is usually required when you apply for a job, and many jobs require different kinds of writing every day.

"If you would not be forgotten as soon as you are dead, either write something worth reading or do things worth writing about."

Benjamin Franklin (1706-1790)

Getting paid to write?

Writing can even become your occupation. A good writer can find success as an author, as a journalist, writing for television or film, or working for publishers. There are specialist technical jobs writing manuals and instruction books, and the Internet has opened up many avenues writing for online publications.

So, get out there and write. Communicate. Be remembered. Your words will outlive you, so make every one of them count!

The difference between the right word and the almost right word is the difference between lightning and the lightning bug."

Mark Twain (1835-1910)

"The pen is mightier than the sword."

Edward Bulwer-Lytton (1803-1873)

J.K. Rowling has become one of the richest women in the world through writing. In 1997 she published Harry Potter and The Philosopher's Stone, *the first of seven blockbuster books about a boy wizard. Rowling came up with the Harry Potter idea at a time when she was struggling to support her young daughter as a single mum. Now, she will never have to worry about money again.*

QUIZ RESULTS

PRACTICING GOOD GRAMMAR
For page 13
1) c
2) a
3) b
4) b

ESSAY EXPERT
For page 35
1) b
2) a
3) b

WRITING TECHNIQUE
For page 26
1) b
2) b
3) b
4) b

A LOVE FOR LITERATURE
For page 39
1) b
2) a and c
3) b

⬤20 THINGS TO REMEMBER

1 Blend the conversational and formal styles of writing to sound intelligent and smooth.

2 Writing should flow in a logical order so it makes sense to whoever is reading it.

3 Enhance writing with sprinkles of strong, colourful words.

4 Preparation is needed before writing can begin.

5 Free write and brainstorm to expand your ideas into useful notes.

6 Organize your notes and research with an outline composed of a main topic, subtopics, supporting information, and facts.

7 When you can, pick a fun and interesting topic that is easy to research.

8 Record all bibliographical information from gathered resources.

9 A thesis statement should be short, compact, and strong.

10 Summarize or paraphrase from your notes and research materials.

11 A persuasive argument is backed up with facts to prove points.

12 Research both sides of an argument even when only writing about one.

13 Even when writing about literature, research can provide insights to the text.

14 Use sources and quotations to strengthen an opinion.

15 Just because creative writing comes from your own ideas doesn't mean it can be slipshod or done quickly without drafting and reworking.

16 Plays written by students aren't blockbuster films with special effects. You have to write things that can be presented, so no flying elephants or impossible transformations!

17 There are many magazines and journals that publish student poetry and short stories, but don't expect to get paid much, if at all.

18 A formal letter should be written clearly and to the point so the reader can quickly understand the reason for writing.

19 A speech should be written how the speaker talks.

20 Use an effective "attention getter" to grab and hold the audience's attention when writing a speech.

FURTHER INFORMATION

BOOKS/GUIDES

Fast Forward Writing: Sue Hackman (Hodder Murray, 2004)

How to Write Dissertations & Project Reports: Kathleen McMillan, Jonathan Weyers (Pearson Education, 2007)

How to Write Essays & Assignments: Kathleen McMillan, Jonathan Weyers (Pearson Education, 2007)

Wordsmith: A Guide to Paragraphs and Essays: Pamela Arlov (Pearson Education, 2008)

WEBSITES

BBC Blast
www.bbc.co.uk/blast/writing
Tips on writing from writers, competitions, upload your own writing, links to other writing websites.

BBC Skillswise
www.bbc.co.uk/skillswise
Improve your grammar, spelling, and writing.

Booktrust
www.booktrust.org.uk/Home
Recommended fiction for children, book awards, book events, competitions, resources for schools.

Poetry Library
www.poetrylibrary.org.uk/education/children
Advice for young poets, details of poetry events, competitons, links to other poetry websites.